Contents

Sweet Hot Chicken Wings

3   **pounds chicken wings, tips removed and split at joints**

³/₄   **cup salsa, plus additional for serving**

²/₃   **cup honey**

¹/₃   **cup soy sauce**

¹/₄   **cup Dijon mustard**

2   **tablespoons vegetable oil**

1   **tablespoon grated fresh ginger**

¹/₂   **teaspoon grated lemon peel**

¹/₂   **teaspoon grated orange peel**

    Celery sticks

    Blue cheese dressing

1. Combine wings, ³/₄ cup salsa, honey, soy sauce, mustard, ginger, lemon peel and orange peel in large bowl; mix well. Marinate, covered, in refrigerator at least 6 hours or overnight.

2. Drain wings; discard marinade. Heat 1 tablespoon oil in large skillet over high heat 1 minute. Add half of wings; cook 3 to 4 minutes or until wings are brown on all sides, turning occasionally. Remove with slotted spoon to **CROCK-POT®** slow cooker. Repeat with remaining 1 tablespoon oil and wings.

3. Cover; cook on HIGH 2 hours. Serve warm with additional salsa, celery and dressing.

Makes about 34 appetizers

Mini Carnitas Tacos

- 1 1/2 **pounds boneless pork loin**
- 1 **onion, finely chopped**
- 1/2 **cup chicken broth**
- 1 **tablespoon chili powder**
- 2 **teaspoons ground cumin**
- 1 **teaspoon dried oregano**
- 1/2 **teaspoon minced canned chipotle peppers in adobo sauce**
- 1/2 **cup pico de gallo**
- 2 **tablespoons chopped fresh cilantro**
- 1/2 **teaspoon salt**
- 12 **(6-inch) corn or flour tortillas**
- 3/4 **cup (3 ounces) shredded sharp Cheddar cheese**
- 3 **tablespoons sour cream**

1. Combine pork, onion, broth, chili powder, cumin, oregano and chipotle peppers in **CROCK-POT®** slow cooker; stir to blend. Cover; cook on LOW 6 hours or on HIGH 3 hours. Pour off excess cooking liquid.

2. Remove pork to large cutting board; shred with two forks. Stir shredded pork, pico de gallo, cilantro and salt into **CROCK-POT®** slow cooker. Cover; keep warm on LOW or WARM setting.

3. Cut three circles from each tortilla with 2-inch biscuit cutter. Top each evenly with pork, cheese and sour cream. Serve warm.

Makes 12 servings

Tip: Carnitas, or "little meats" in Spanish, are a festive way to spice up any gathering. Carnitas traditionally include a large amount of lard, but slow cooking makes the dish healthier by eliminating the need to add lard, oil or fat, while keeping the meat tender and delicious.

Soy-Braised Chicken Wings

- ¼ **cup dry sherry**
- ¼ **cup soy sauce**
- 3 **tablespoons sugar**
- 2 **tablespoons cornstarch**
- 2 **tablespoons minced garlic, divided**
- 2 **teaspoons red pepper flakes**
- 12 **chicken wings (about 2½ pounds), tips removed and cut at joints**
- 2 **tablespoons vegetable oil**
- 3 **green onions, cut into 1-inch pieces**
- ¼ **cup chicken broth**
- 1 **teaspoon sesame oil**
- 1 **tablespoon sesame seeds, toasted***

*To toast sesame seeds, place in small skillet. Shake skillet over medium-low heat about 3 minutes or until seeds begin to pop and turn golden. Remove from heat.

1. Combine sherry, soy sauce, sugar, cornstarch, 1 tablespoon garlic and red pepper flakes in large bowl; mix well. Reserve ¼ cup marinade in separate bowl. Stir wings into remaining marinade. Cover; marinate in refrigerator overnight, turning once or twice.

2. Drain wings; discard marinade. Heat 1 tablespoon vegetable oil in large skillet over high heat 1 minute. Add half of wings; cook 3 to 4 minutes or until wings are brown on all sides, turning occasionally. Remove with slotted spoon to **CROCK-POT®** slow cooker. Repeat with remaining vegetable oil and wings.

3. Add remaining 1 tablespoon garlic and green onions to skillet; cook and stir 30 seconds. Stir in broth and pour over wings. Cover; cook on HIGH 2 hours.

4. Remove wings to large serving platter with slotted spoon. Add sesame oil to reserved marinade; mix well. Pour over wings; sprinkle with sesame seeds.

Makes 2 dozen wings

Feta and Mint Spread

- 1/2 cup plain Greek yogurt*
- 3 ounces feta cheese, crumbled
- 2 ounces cream cheese, cubed
- 2 tablespoons extra virgin olive oil
- 1 small clove garlic, crushed to a paste
  Baked Pita Chips (recipe follows)
- 1 tablespoon chopped fresh mint
- 1/2 teaspoon grated fresh lemon peel

Greek yogurt is yogurt from which much of the liquid (or "whey") has been drained before use. It is available in most major supermarkets. To make your own, place 1/2 cup plain yogurt in a small colander lined with several layers of damp cheesecloth. Suspend over a large bowl and refrigerate overnight.

1. Coat inside of **CROCK-POT® LITTLE DIPPER®** slow cooker with nonstick cooking spray. Add yogurt, feta cheese, cream cheese, oil and garlic; mix well. Cover; heat 1 hour or until cheese is melted.

2. Meanwhile, prepare Baked Pita Chips.

3. Stir in mint and lemon peel. Serve with Baked Pita Chips.

Makes 12 servings

Baked Pita Chips

        3 **pita bread rounds**
        1 **tablespoon extra virgin olive oil**
    $1/2$ **teaspoon dried oregano**
    $1/4$ **teaspoon ground cumin**
    $1/8$ **teaspoon salt**

1. Preheat oven to 375°F. Spray large baking sheet with nonstick cooking spray.

2. Brush one side of each pita round with oil. Sprinkle with oregano, cumin and salt. Cut each pita round into 12 wedges. Place on prepared baking sheet seasoned side up. Bake 8 minutes or until lightly browned. Cool.

Makes **36** *chips*

Chipotle Chili Con Queso Dip

- 10 **ounces pasteurized process cheese product, cubed**
- 1/4 **cup mild chunky salsa**
- 1/2 **canned chipotle peppers in adobo sauce, finely chopped**
- 1/2 **teaspoon Worcestershire sauce**
- 1/8 **teaspoon chili powder**
- **Pretzels**

1. Coat inside of **CROCK-POT® LITTLE DIPPER®** slow cooker. Combine cheese product, salsa, chipotle peppers, Worcestershire sauce and chili powder in **CROCK-POT® LITTLE DIPPER®** slow cooker. Cover; heat 1 hour.

2. Stir well. Replace cover; heat 30 minutes or until cheese product is melted. Stir until smooth. Serve with pretzels.

Makes 1 1/2 cups

Pancetta Horseradish Dip

- **3 slices pancetta**
- **8 ounces cream cheese, cubed**
- **³/₄ cup (3 ounces) shredded Swiss cheese**
- **¹/₄ cup whipping cream**
- **¹/₄ cup chopped green onions, plus additional for topping**
- **1 tablespoon prepared horseradish, drained**
- **1 teaspoon Worcestershire sauce**
- **¹/₂ teaspoon Dijon mustard**
- **Potato chips**

1. Heat small skillet over medium heat. Add pancetta; cook 4 minutes or until crisp, turning occasionally. Drain on paper towels. Let cool; crumble and set aside.

2. Coat inside of **CROCK-POT® LITTLE DIPPER®** slow cooker with nonstick cooking spray. Add cream cheese, Swiss cheese, cream, ¹/₄ cup green onions, horseradish, Worcestershire sauce and mustard. Cover; heat 1 hour. Stir. Cover; heat 30 minutes or until cheese is melted.

3. Stir in all but 2 teaspoons pancetta. Sprinkle remaining pancetta and additional green onions on top. Serve with potato chips.

Makes about 1¹/₂ cups

Chesapeake Bay Crab Dip

- 1 can (6$^1/_2$ ounces) crabmeat, well drained
- 3 ounces cream cheese, cubed
- $^1/_3$ cup sour cream
- 3 tablespoons mayonnaise
- 2 tablespoons finely chopped onion
- $^1/_2$ teaspoon Chesapeake Bay seasoning
- $^1/_4$ teaspoon hot pepper sauce
- 1 tablespoon chopped fresh chives
  Multi-grain crackers and baby carrots

1. Coat inside of **CROCK-POT® LITTLE DIPPER®** slow cooker with nonstick cooking spray. Pick out and discard any shell or cartilage from crabmeat. Add crabmeat, cream cheese, sour cream, mayonnaise, onion, Chesapeake Bay seasoning and hot pepper sauce; stir until blended.

2. Cover; heat 1 hour. Stir well. Cover; heat 30 minutes. Stir in chives. Serve with crackers and carrots.

Makes about 1$^1/_2$ cups

Curried Snack Mix

     3 tablespoons butter
     2 tablespoons packed light brown sugar
 1 1/2 teaspoons hot curry powder
   1/4 teaspoon ground cumin
   1/4 teaspoon salt
     2 cups rice cereal squares
     1 cup walnut halves
     1 cup dried cranberries

1. Melt butter in large skillet. Add brown sugar, curry powder, cumin and salt; mix well. Add cereal, walnuts and cranberries; stir to coat. Remove mixture to **CROCK-POT®** slow cooker.

2. Cover; cook on LOW 3 hours. Uncover; cook on LOW 30 minutes.

Makes 16 servings

Spicy Cheddar Dip

- 4 **ounces cream cheese, cubed**
- 1 **cup (4 ounces) shredded extra sharp Cheddar cheese**
- 2 **slices bacon, crisp-cooked and chopped**
- 1/2 **jalapeño pepper, finely chopped***
- 1/2 **teaspoon hot pepper sauce**
- 3 **tablespoons sour cream**
  Tortilla chips and/or pretzel sticks

*Jalapeño peppers can sting and irritate the skin, so wear rubber gloves when handling peppers and do not touch your eyes.

1. Coat inside of **CROCK-POT® LITTLE DIPPER®** slow cooker with nonstick cooking spray. Add cream cheese, Cheddar cheese, bacon, jalapeño pepper and hot pepper sauce; stir to blend.

2. Cover; heat 1 hour. Stir in sour cream. Cover; heat 30 minutes or until heated through and cheese is melted. Serve with tortilla chips and/or pretzel sticks.

Makes about 1 1/2 cups

S'mores Fondue

- **4 ounces semisweet chocolate chips**
- **¹/₂ jar (about 3 ounces) marshmallow creme**
- **3 tablespoons half-and-half**
- **¹/₂ teaspoon vanilla**
- **¹/₂ cup mini marshmallows**
- **Bananas, strawberries, chocolate-covered pretzels, graham crackers and/or sliced apples**

1. Combine chocolate chips, marshmallow creme and half-and-half in medium saucepan. Cook over medium heat 2 minutes or until melted and smooth, stirring constantly. Remove from heat. Stir in vanilla.

2. Coat inside of **CROCK-POT® LITTLE DIPPER®** slow cooker with nonstick cooking spray. Fill with warm fondue. Sprinkle with marshmallows. Serve with fruit, pretzels and graham crackers.

Makes 1¹/₂ cups

Chocolate Orange Fondue

- ¹/₂ **cup whipping cream**
- 1¹/₂ **tablespoons butter**
- 6 **ounces 60 to 70% bittersweet chocolate, coarsely chopped**
- ¹/₃ **cup orange liqueur**
- ³/₄ **teaspoon vanilla**
- **Marshmallows, strawberries and pound cake cubes**

1. Bring cream and butter to a boil in medium saucepan over medium heat. Remove from heat. Stir in chocolate, liqueur and vanilla until chocolate is melted. Place over medium-low heat; cook and stir 2 minutes until smooth.

2. Coat inside of **CROCK-POT® LITTLE DIPPER®** slow cooker with nonstick cooking spray. Fill with warm fondue. Serve with marshmallows, strawberries and pound cake cubes.

Makes 1¹/₂ cups

Bagna Cauda

- $3/4$ **cup olive oil**
- 6 **tablespoons butter, softened**
- 12 **anchovy fillets, drained**
- 6 **cloves garlic**
- $1/8$ **teaspoon red pepper flakes**

    Optional dippers: sugar snap peas, bell pepper slices, green onions, cucumber spears, zucchini spears, carrot sticks and/ or bread sticks

1. Place oil, butter, anchovies, garlic and red pepper flakes in food processor or blender; process 30 seconds or until smooth. Heat medium saucepan over medium heat. Pour oil mixture into saucepan; bring to a boil. Reduce heat to medium-low; simmer 5 minutes.

2. Coat inside of **CROCK-POT® LITTLE DIPPER®** slow cooker with nonstick cooking spray. Fill with warm dip. Serve with desired dippers.

Makes 1$1/3$ cups

Maple-Glazed Meatballs

- 1¹/₂ **cups ketchup**
- 1 **cup maple syrup**
- ¹/₃ **cup soy sauce**
- 1 **tablespoon quick-cooking tapioca**
- 1¹/₂ **teaspoons ground allspice**
- 1 **teaspoon dry mustard**
- 2 **packages (about 16 ounces *each*) frozen fully cooked meatballs, partially thawed and separated**
- 1 **can (20 ounces) pineapple chunks in juice, drained**

1. Combine ketchup, maple syrup, soy sauce, tapioca, allspice and dry mustard in **CROCK-POT®** slow cooker; stir to blend. Carefully stir meatballs and pineapple chunks into ketchup mixture.

2. Cover; cook on LOW 5 to 6 hours. Stir before serving. Serve warm; insert cocktail picks, if desired.

Makes about 48 meatballs

Coconut Rice Pudding

- 2 **cups water**
- 1 **cup uncooked converted long grain rice**
- 1 **tablespoon unsalted butter**
  - **Pinch salt**
- 2¼ **cups evaporated milk**
- 1 **can (14 ounces) cream of coconut**
- ½ **cup golden raisins**
- 3 **egg yolks, beaten**
  - **Grated peel of 2 limes**
- 1 **teaspoon vanilla**
  - **Toasted shredded coconut (optional)***

*To toast coconut, spread evenly on ungreased baking sheet. Toast in preheated 350°F degree oven 5 to 7 minutes or until light golden brown, stirring occasionally.

1. Place water, rice, butter and salt in medium saucepan. Bring to a boil over high heat, stirring frequently. Reduce heat to low. Cover; cook 10 to 12 minutes. Remove from heat. Let stand, covered, 5 minutes.

2. Meanwhile, coat inside of **CROCK-POT®** slow cooker with nonstick cooking spray. Add evaporated milk, cream of coconut, raisins, egg yolks, lime peel and vanilla; mix well. Add rice; stir until blended.

3. Cover; cook on LOW 4 hours or on HIGH 2 hours. Stir every 30 minutes, if possible. Pudding will thicken as it cools. Garnish with shredded coconut.

Makes 6 servings

Apple-Cranberry Crêpes

- 1 **baking apple, such as Gala or Jonathan, peeled, cored and cut into 6 wedges**
- 1 **tart apple, such as Granny Smith, peeled, cored and cut into 6 wedges**
- $1/4$ **cup dried sweetened cranberries or cherries**
- 2 **tablespoons lemon juice**
- $1/2$ **teaspoon plus $1/8$ teaspoon ground cinnamon, divided**
- $1/8$ **teaspoon ground nutmeg**
- $1/8$ **teaspoon ground cloves or allspice**
- 1 **tablespoon butter**
- $1/4$ **cup orange juice**
- 1 **tablespoon sugar**
- $3/4$ **teaspoon cornstarch**
- $1/4$ **teaspoon almond extract**
- 4 **prepared crêpes**
- 1 **cup vanilla ice cream**

1. Coat inside of **CROCK-POT®** slow cooker with nonstick cooking spray. Place apples, cranberries, lemon juice, $1/2$ teaspoon cinnamon, nutmeg and cloves in **CROCK-POT®** slow cooker; toss to coat. Cover; cook on LOW 2 hours. Stir butter into apple mixture just until melted.

2. Stir orange juice, sugar, cornstarch and almond extract in small bowl until cornstarch dissolves. Stir into apple mixture in **CROCK-POT®** slow cooker. Turn **CROCK-POT®** slow cooker to HIGH. Cover; cook on HIGH 15 minutes or until sauce thickens.

3. Place one crêpe on each of four dessert plates. Spoon apple mixture evenly down center of each crêpe. Fold edges over; turn crêpes with seam side down on plates. Sprinkle with remaining $1/8$ teaspoon cinnamon. Microwave filled crêpes according to package directions, if desired. Serve with ice cream.

Makes 4 servings

Tip: Look for prepared crêpes in the produce section of the supermarket.

Mexican Hot Pot

- 1 tablespoon canola oil
- 1 medium onion, chopped
- 3 cloves garlic, minced
- 2 teaspoons red pepper flakes
- 2 teaspoons dried oregano
- 1 teaspoon ground cumin
- 1 can (28 ounces) whole tomatoes, drained and chopped
- 2 cups corn
- 1 can (about 15 ounces) chickpeas, rinsed and drained
- 1 can (about 15 ounces) pinto beans, rinsed and drained
- 1 cup water
- 6 cups shredded iceberg lettuce

1. Heat oil in large skillet over medium-high heat. Add onion and garlic; cook and stir 5 minutes. Add red pepper flakes, oregano and cumin; mix well. Remove onion and garlic mixture to **CROCK-POT®** slow cooker.

2. Stir in tomatoes, corn, chickpeas, beans and water. Cover; cook on LOW 7 to 8 hours or on HIGH 2 to 3 hours. Top each serving with shredded lettuce.

Makes 6 servings

Saag Paneer

- 2 onions, finely chopped
- 8 cloves garlic, minced
- 1 teaspoon ground coriander
- 1 teaspoon ground cumin
- $1/2$ teaspoon pumpkin pie spice
- $1/2$ teaspoon ground cardamom
- $1/2$ teaspoon salt
- 2 packages (10 ounces *each*) frozen chopped spinach, thawed and squeezed dry
- 2 packages (9 ounces *each*) frozen chopped creamed spinach, thawed
- 2 tablespoons butter
- 8 ounces paneer, cut into $1/2$-inch cubes*
- Pita bread rounds, cut into wedges

*Paneer is a firm, fresh cheese used in South Asian cuisines. Substitute any firm white cheese or extra firm tofu.

1. Combine onions, garlic, coriander, cumin, pumpkin pie spice, cardamom and salt in **CROCK-POT®** slow cooker; stir to blend. Add spinach, creamed spinach and butter. Cover; cook on LOW $4^{1}/_{2}$ to 5 hours.

2. Add paneer. Cover; cook on LOW 30 minutes or until paneer is heated through. Serve with pita wedges.

Makes 10 servings

Lentils with Walnuts

3 cups chicken broth
1 cup dried brown lentils, rinsed and sorted
1 small onion or large shallot, chopped
1 stalk celery, trimmed and chopped
1 large carrot, chopped
$1/4$ teaspoon dried thyme
Salt and black pepper
$1/4$ cup chopped walnuts

1. Combine broth, lentils, onion, celery, carrot and thyme in **CROCK-POT®** slow cooker; stir to blend. Cover; cook on HIGH 3 hours or until lentils absorb most of broth.

2. Season with salt and pepper. Spoon lentils into serving bowls; sprinkle with walnuts.

Makes 4 to 6 servings

Serving Suggestion: Top each dish with cooked bacon or ham.

Asparagus and Cheese

$1^1/_2$ **pounds fresh asparagus, trimmed**

2 **cups crushed saltine crackers**

1 **can ($10^3/_4$ ounces) condensed cream of asparagus soup, undiluted**

1 **can ($10^3/_4$ ounces) condensed cream of chicken or cream of celery soup, undiluted**

4 **ounces American cheese, cubed**

$^2/_3$ **cup slivered almonds**

1 **egg**

Black pepper

Combine asparagus, crackers, soups, cheese, almonds and egg in **CROCK-POT®** slow cooker; toss to coat. Cover; cook on HIGH 3 to $3^1/_2$ hours. Season with pepper.

Makes 4 to 6 servings

Tip: Cooking times are guidelines. **CROCK-POT®** slow cookers, just like ovens, cook differently depending on a variety of factors. For example, cooking times will be longer at higher altitudes. You may need to slightly adjust cooking times.

Spring Pea and Mint Broth Soup

8 cups water

3 carrots, cut into ¹/₄-inch slices

2 onions, coarsely chopped

2 to 3 leeks, cleaned well and coarsely chopped

2 stalks celery, cut into ¹/₄-inch slices

1 bunch fresh mint

3 to 4 cups fresh spring peas or 1 bag (32 ounces) frozen peas

1 tablespoon fresh lemon juice

   Salt and black pepper

   Sour cream

1. Combine water, carrots, onions, leeks, celery and mint in **CROCK-POT®** slow cooker; stir to blend. Cover; cook on HIGH 5 hours.

2. Strain broth. Return to **CROCK-POT®** slow cooker. Discard solids. Add peas and lemon juice. Cover; cook on LOW 4 to 5 hours or on HIGH 2 to 3 hours.

3. Season with salt and pepper. Ladle soup into bowls; top with sour cream.

Makes 6 to 8 servings

Easy Vegetarian Vegetable Bean Soup

3 cans (about 14 ounces *each*) vegetable broth

2 cups cubed unpeeled red potatoes

2 cups sliced leeks, white part only (about 3 medium)

1 can (about 14 ounces) diced tomatoes

1 medium onion, chopped

1 cup chopped or shredded cabbage

1 cup sliced celery

1 cup sliced carrots

3 cloves garlic, chopped

$\frac{1}{8}$ teaspoon dried rosemary

1 can (about 15 ounces) white beans, drained

Salt and black pepper

1. Combine broth, potatoes, leeks, tomatoes, onion, cabbage, celery, carrots, garlic and rosemary in **CROCK-POT®** slow cooker; stir to blend. Cover; cook on LOW 8 hours.

2. Stir in beans. Season with salt and pepper. Cover; cook on LOW 30 minutes or until beans are heated through.

Makes **10** *servings*

Orange-Spice Glazed Carrots

- **1 package (32 ounces) baby carrots**
- **$^1/_2$ cup packed light brown sugar**
- **$^1/_2$ cup orange juice**
- **3 tablespoons butter**
- **$^3/_4$ teaspoon ground cinnamon**
- **$^1/_4$ teaspoon ground nutmeg**
- **$^1/_4$ cup cold water**
- **2 tablespoons cornstarch**
- **Orange peel (optional)**
- **Chopped fresh Italian parsley (optional)**

1. Combine carrots, brown sugar, orange juice, butter, cinnamon and nutmeg in **CROCK-POT®** slow cooker; stir to blend. Cover; cook on LOW $3^1/_2$ to 4 hours.

2. Spoon carrots into large serving bowl; keep warm. Turn **CROCK-POT®** slow cooker to HIGH.

3. Stir water into cornstarch in small bowl until smooth; whisk into cooking liquid. Cover; cook on HIGH 15 minutes or until thickened. Spoon over carrots. Garnish with orange peel and parsley.

Makes 6 servings

Scallop and Corn Chowder

- **6 tablespoons butter, divided**
- **1 bunch leeks, diced**
- **3/4 pound pancetta, diced**
- **5 small Yukon Gold potatoes, diced**
- **5 1/4 cups fish broth**
- **2 cups corn**
- **1 tablespoon minced fresh thyme**
- **4 tablespoons all-purpose flour**
- **1 pound sea scallops, quartered**
- **2 cups whipping cream**
- **Black pepper**
- **Sprigs fresh thyme (optional)**

1. Heat 2 tablespoons butter in large skillet over medium-high heat. Add leeks; cook and stir 5 to 7 minutes or until softened and just beginning to brown. Remove to **CROCK-POT®** slow cooker.

2. Add pancetta to same skillet; cook and stir 5 to 7 minutes or until lightly browned. Remove to **CROCK-POT®** slow cooker. Add potatoes, broth, corn and minced thyme. Cover; cook on LOW 4 to 6 hours or on HIGH 2 to 3 hours.

3. Combine remaining 4 tablespoons butter and flour in large saucepan; cook and stir 5 minutes over medium heat to make roux. Stir in 2 cups broth from **CROCK-POT®** slow cooker until fully combined. Stir mixture back into **CROCK-POT®** slow cooker until blended. Stir in scallops. Cover; cook on HIGH 10 minutes or until scallops are just cooked through.

4. Stir in cream; season with pepper. Garnish with thyme sprigs.

Makes 6 to 8 servings

Pesto Rice and Beans

1 **can (about 15 ounces) Great Northern beans, rinsed and drained**
1 **can (about 14 ounces) vegetable broth**
³/₄ **cup uncooked converted long grain rice**
1¹/₂ **cups frozen cut green beans, thawed and drained**
¹/₂ **cup prepared pesto**
Grated Parmesan cheese

1. Combine Great Northern beans, broth and rice in **CROCK-POT®** slow cooker; stir to blend. Cover; cook on LOW 2 hours.

2. Stir in green beans. Cover; cook on LOW 1 hour or until rice and beans are tender.

3. Turn off heat. Stir in pesto and cheese. Let stand, covered, 5 minutes or until cheese is melted. Serve immediately.

Makes 8 servings

Raspberry-Balsamic Glazed Meatballs

- 1 **bag (2 pounds) frozen fully cooked meatballs**
- 1 **cup raspberry preserves**
- 3 **tablespoons sugar**
- 3 **tablespoons balsamic vinegar**
- 1 **tablespoon plus 1¹/₂ teaspoons Worcestershire sauce**
- ¹/₄ **teaspoon red pepper flakes**
- 1 **tablespoon grated fresh ginger (optional)**
   Sliced green onions (optional)

1. Coat inside of **CROCK-POT®** slow cooker with nonstick cooking spray. Add meatballs.

2. Combine preserves, sugar, vinegar, Worcestershire sauce and red pepper flakes in small microwavable bowl. Microwave on HIGH 45 seconds; stir. Microwave 15 seconds or until melted. Reserve ¹/₂ cup glaze in refrigerator. Pour glaze mixture over meatballs; stir until well coated. Cover; cook on LOW 5 hours or on HIGH 2¹/₂ hours.

3. Stir in reserved glaze and ginger, if desired. Cook, uncovered, on HIGH 15 to 20 minutes or until thickened. Top with green onions, if desired.

Makes about 16 servings

Easiest Three-Cheese Fondue

2 cups (8 ounces) shredded Cheddar cheese
³/₄ cup milk
1 package (3 ounces) cream cheese, cut into cubes
¹/₂ cup crumbled blue cheese
¹/₄ cup finely chopped onion
1 tablespoon all-purpose flour
1 tablespoon butter
2 cloves garlic, minced
4 to 6 drops hot pepper sauce
¹/₈ teaspoon ground red pepper
Breadsticks and assorted cut-up fresh vegetables

1. Combine Cheddar cheese, milk, cream cheese, blue cheese, onion, flour, butter, garlic, hot pepper sauce and ground red pepper in **CROCK-POT®** slow cooker. Cover; cook on LOW 2 to 2¹/₂ hours, stirring halfway through cooking time.

2. Turn **CROCK-POT®** slow cooker to HIGH. Cover; cook on HIGH 1 to 1¹/₂ hours or until heated through. Serve with breadsticks and vegetables.

Makes 8 servings

Cranberry-Barbecue Chicken Wings

- **3** **pounds chicken wings, tips removed and split at joints**
  Salt and black pepper
- **1** **jar (12 ounces) cranberry-orange relish**
- **¹/₂** **cup barbecue sauce**
- **2** **tablespoons quick-cooking tapioca**
- **1** **tablespoon prepared mustard**

1. Preheat broiler. Place wings on rack in broiler pan; season with salt and pepper. Broil 4 to 5 inches from heat 10 to 12 minutes or until browned, turning once. Remove wings to **CROCK-POT®** slow cooker using slotted spoon.

2. Combine relish, barbecue sauce, tapioca and mustard in medium bowl; stir to blend. Pour over wings. Cover; cook on LOW 4 to 5 hours.

Makes 6 servings

Mexican Cheese Soup

- 1 **pound ground beef**
- 1 **pound pasteurized process cheese product, cubed**
- 1 **can (about 15 ounces) kidney beans, rinsed and drained**
- 1 **can (about 14 ounces) diced tomatoes with mild green chiles**
- 1 **can (about 14 ounces) stewed tomatoes, undrained**
- 1 **can (8³/₄ ounces) corn**
- 1 **envelope taco seasoning**
- 1 **jalapeño pepper, seeded and diced (optional)***
  Tortilla chips (optional)

*Jalapeño peppers can sting and irritate the skin, so wear rubber gloves when handling peppers and do not touch your eyes.

1. Coat inside of **CROCK-POT®** slow cooker with nonstick cooking spray. Brown beef in large skillet 6 to 8 minutes, stirring to break up meat. Remove to **CROCK-POT®** slow cooker using slotted spoon.

2. Add cheese product, beans, tomatoes with chiles, stewed tomatoes, corn, taco seasoning and jalapeño pepper, if desired; stir to blend. Cover; cook on LOW 4 to 5 hours or on HIGH 3 hours. Serve with tortilla chips, if desired.

Makes 6 to 8 servings

Chunky Veggie Dip ⌒

- 1 red bell pepper, chopped
- 1 green bell pepper, chopped
- 1/2 onion, finely chopped
- 1 stalk celery, chopped
- 2 tablespoons water
- 1/8 teaspoon red pepper flakes
- 1/4 cup milk
- 3/4 teaspoon cornstarch
- 1 cup (4 ounces) shredded sharp Cheddar cheese
- 2 ounces cream cheese
- 1 jar (4 ounces) diced pimientos
- 3/4 teaspoon salt
  Tortilla chips

1. Coat inside of **CROCK-POT®** slow cooker with nonstick cooking spray. Add bell peppers, onion, celery, water and red pepper flakes. Cover; cook on LOW 3 hours or until celery is tender.

2. Stir milk into cornstarch in small bowl until smooth; whisk into bell pepper mixture. Stir in Cheddar cheese and cream cheese, pressing down on cream cheese with rubber spatula until well blended. Stir in pimientos and salt. Cover; cook on LOW 15 minutes or until thickened. Serve with tortilla chips.

Makes **3** *cups*

Variation: Use soft corn tortillas instead of chips. Cut each tortilla into six wedges and bake in a single layer on a baking sheet at 350°F for 10 minutes. Cool completely before serving.

Brats in Beer

1¹/₂ **pounds bratwurst (5 to 6 links)**
   1 **can (12 ounces) amber ale or beer**
   1 **onion, thinly sliced**
   2 **tablespoons packed brown sugar**
   2 **tablespoons dry red wine or cider vinegar**
     Spicy brown mustard
     Cocktail rye bread

1. Combine bratwurst, ale, onion, brown sugar and vinegar in **CROCK-POT®** slow cooker. Cover; cook on LOW 4 to 5 hours.

2. Remove bratwurst from cooking liquid. Cut into ¹/₂-inch-thick slices.

3. To make mini open-faced sandwiches, spread mustard on cocktail rye bread. Top with bratwurst slices and onion.

Makes 30 to 36 appetizers

Tip: Choose a light-colored beer when cooking brats. Hearty ales can leave the meat tasting slightly bitter.

Reuben Dip

- **1 jar or bag (about 32 ounces) sauerkraut, drained**
- **2 cups (8 ounces) shredded Swiss cheese**
- **3 packages (2½ ounces *each*) corned beef, shredded**
- **½ cup (1 stick) butter, melted**
- **1 egg, beaten**
- **Cocktail rye bread**

Combine sauerkraut, cheese, corned beef, butter and egg in **CROCK-POT®** slow cooker. Cover; cook on HIGH 2 hours. Serve with bread.

Makes 12 servings

Parmesan Potato Wedges

- **2 pounds red potatoes, cut into ½-inch wedges**
- **¼ cup finely chopped yellow onion**
- **1½ teaspoons dried oregano**
- **½ teaspoon salt**
- **¼ teaspoon black pepper**
- **2 tablespoons butter, cubed**
- **¼ cup grated Parmesan cheese**

Layer potatoes, onion, oregano, salt and pepper in **CROCK-POT®** slow cooker; dot with butter. Cover; cook on HIGH 4 hours. Remove potatoes to large serving platter; sprinkle with cheese.

Makes 6 servings

Reuben Dip

Red Pepper Relish

- 4 large red bell peppers, cut into thin strips
- 2 small Vidalia or other sweet onions, thinly sliced
- 6 tablespoons cider vinegar
- 1/4 cup packed brown sugar
- 2 tablespoons vegetable oil
- 2 tablespoons honey
- 1/2 teaspoon salt
- 1/2 teaspoon dried thyme
- 1/2 teaspoon red pepper flakes
- 1/2 teaspoon black pepper
- 2 baguettes, sliced and toasted

Combine bell peppers, onions, vinegar, brown sugar, oil, honey, salt, thyme, red pepper flakes and black pepper in **CROCK-POT®** slow cooker; mix well. Cover; cook on LOW 4 hours. Serve on toasted baguette slices.

Makes 8 servings

Tropical Chicken Wings

       3 **pounds chicken wings, tips removed and split at joints**
         Salt and black pepper
       1 **jar (12 ounces) pineapple preserves**
    $^1/_2$ **cup chopped green onions**
    $^1/_2$ **cup soy sauce**
       3 **tablespoons lime juice**
       2 **tablespoons honey**
       1 **tablespoon minced garlic**
       2 **teaspoons spicy chili sauce**
    $^1/_4$ **teaspoon ground allspice**
       1 **tablespoon toasted sesame seeds***
         Lime slices (optional)

*To toast sesame seeds, spread in small skillet. Shake skillet over medium heat 2 minutes or until seeds begin to pop and turn golden brown.

1. Preheat broiler. Place wings on rack in broiler pan; season with salt and pepper. Broil 4 to 5 inches from heat 10 to 12 minutes or until browned, turning once. Remove wings to **CROCK-POT®** slow cooker using slotted spoon.

2. Combine preserves, green onions, soy sauce, lime juice, honey, garlic, chili sauce and allspice in medium bowl; stir to blend. Pour over wings. Cover; cook on LOW 3 to 4 hours. Sprinkle with sesame seeds. Garnish with lime slices.

Makes 6 to 8 servings

Easy Dirty Rice

- $^1/_2$ **pound bulk Italian sausage**
- 2 **cups water**
- 1 **cup uncooked long grain rice**
- 1 **large onion, finely chopped**
- 1 **large green bell pepper, finely chopped**
- $^1/_2$ **cup finely chopped celery**
- $1^1/_2$ **teaspoons salt**
- $^1/_2$ **teaspoon ground red pepper**
- $^1/_2$ **cup chopped fresh Italian parsley**

1. Brown sausage in large skillet over medium-high heat 6 to 8 minutes, stirring to break up meat. Remove sausage to **CROCK-POT®** slow cooker using slotted spoon.

2. Stir in water, rice, onion, bell pepper, celery, salt and ground red pepper. Cover; cook on LOW 2 hours. Stir in parsley.

Makes 4 servings

Tailgating

Moroccan-Spiced Chicken Wings

- 1 tablespoon olive oil
- 5 pounds chicken wings, tips removed and split at joints
- 1/4 cup orange juice
- 3 tablespoons tomato paste
- 2 teaspoons ground cumin
- 1 teaspoon salt
- 1 teaspoon curry powder
- 1 teaspoon ground turmeric
- 1/2 teaspoon ground ginger
- 1/2 teaspoon ground cinnamon

1. Heat oil in large skillet over medium-high heat. Add wings in batches; cook 6 minutes or until browned on all sides. Remove wings to **CROCK-POT®** slow cooker using slotted spoon.

2. Combine orange juice, tomato paste, cumin, salt, curry powder, turmeric, ginger and cinnamon in large bowl; stir to blend. Pour over wings. Cover; cook on LOW 6 to 7 hours or on HIGH 3 to 3 1/2 hours.

Makes 8 to 10 servings

Pizza Fondue

- $1/2$ **pound bulk Italian sausage**
- 1 **cup chopped onion**
- 2 **jars (26 ounces** *each***) meatless pasta sauce**
- 4 **ounces thinly sliced ham, finely chopped**
- 1 **package (3 ounces) sliced pepperoni, finely chopped**
- $1/4$ **teaspoon red pepper flakes**
- 1 **pound mozzarella cheese, cut into** $3/4$**-inch cubes**
- 1 **loaf Italian or French bread, cut into 1-inch cubes**

1. Brown sausage and onion in large skillet over medium-high heat 6 to 8 minutes, stirring to break up meat. Remove sausage mixture to **CROCK-POT®** slow cooker using slotted spoon.

2. Stir in pasta sauce, ham, pepperoni and red pepper flakes. Cover; cook on LOW 3 to 4 hours. Serve with cheese and bread cubes.

Makes 20 to 25 servings

Fiesta Dip

8 ounces canned refried beans

$^1/_2$ cup (2 ounces) shredded Cheddar cheese, plus additional for garnish

$^1/_3$ cup chopped green chile pepper*

$^1/_4$ cup salsa

Tortilla or corn chips

Chopped fresh tomatoes

Chile peppers can sting and irritate the skin, so wear rubber gloves when handling peppers and do not touch your eyes.

Combine beans, $^1/_2$ cup cheese, chile pepper and salsa in **CROCK-POT® LITTLE DIPPER®** slow cooker. Cover; heat 45 minutes or until cheese is melted, stirring occasionally. Serve on tortilla chips. Garnish with tomatoes and additional cheese.

Makes 16 servings

Best Asian-Style Ribs

2 full racks baby back pork ribs, split into 3 sections *each*

6 ounces hoisin sauce

$^1/_2$ cup maraschino cherries, drained

$^1/_2$ cup rice wine vinegar

2 tablespoons minced fresh ginger

Combine ribs, hoisin sauce, cherries, vinegar and ginger in **CROCK-POT®** slow cooker. Cover; cook on LOW 6 to 7 hours or on HIGH 3 to $3^1/_2$ hours.

Makes 6 to 8 servings

Fiesta Dip

Spiced Beer Fondue

- **2 tablespoons butter**
- **2 tablespoons all-purpose flour**
- **1 can (8 ounces) light-colored beer, such as ale or lager**
- **¹/₂ cup half-and-half**
- **1 cup (4 ounces) shredded smoked gouda cheese**
- **2 teaspoons coarse grain mustard**
- **1 teaspoon Worcestershire sauce**
- **¹/₈ teaspoon salt**
- **¹/₈ teaspoon ground red pepper**
- **Dash ground nutmeg (optional)**
- **Apple slices and cooked potato wedges**

1. Melt butter in medium saucepan over medium heat. Sprinkle with flour; whisk until smooth. Stir in beer and half-and-half; bring to a boil. Cook and stir 2 minutes. Stir in cheese, mustard, Worcestershire sauce, salt and ground red pepper; cook and stir until cheese is melted.

2. Coat inside of **CROCK-POT® LITTLE DIPPER®** slow cooker with nonstick cooking spray. Fill with warm fondue. Sprinkle with nutmeg, if desired. Serve with apples and potatoes.

Makes 1¹/₂ cups

Chunky Pinto Bean Dip

- 1 tablespoon olive oil
- 2 cloves garlic, minced
- $1/2$ teaspoon ground cumin
- 1 can (about 10 ounces) diced tomatoes with mild green chiles
- $1/2$ can (about 15 ounces) pinto beans, rinsed and drained
- 2 tablespoons whipping cream
- $1/2$ cup (2 ounces) shredded sharp Cheddar cheese
- $1/4$ cup chopped fresh cilantro

1. Heat oil in medium saucepan over medium heat. Add garlic and cumin; cook and stir 15 seconds.

2. Drain tomatoes with chiles, reserving $1/4$ canning liquid. Add tomatoes with chiles and reserved liquid to saucepan. Stir in beans.

3. Increase heat to medium-high. Bring to a boil and cook 1 minute. Reduce heat to medium-low. Partially mash with potato masher. Remove from heat. Stir in whipping cream, cheese and cilantro until cheese is melted.

4. Coat inside of **CROCK-POT® LITTLE DIPPER®** slow cooker with nonstick cooking spray. Fill with prepared dip.

Makes 1³/₄ cups

Index